DATE DUE

Demco, Inc. 38-293

Words from the Garden

Isobel Carlson

summersdale

WORDS FROM THE GARDEN
Copyright © Isobel Carlson 2008

Summersdale Publishers Ltd
46 West Street
Chichester
West Sussex
PO19 1RP
UK

www.summersdale.com

Printed and bound by Tien Wah Press, Singapore

ISBN: 1-84024-653-7
ISBN 13: 978-1-84024-653-7

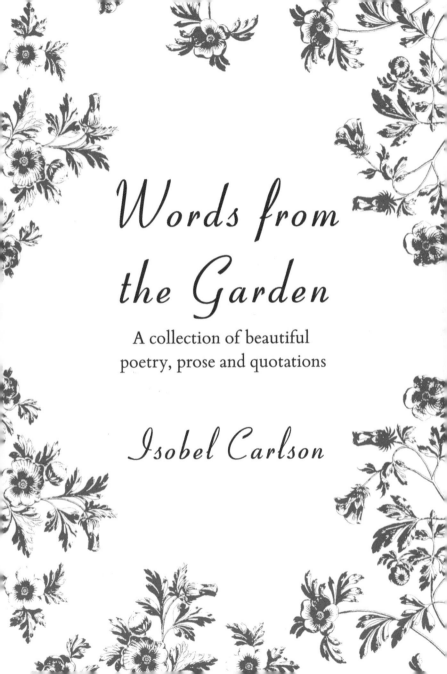

Words from the Garden

A collection of beautiful
poetry, prose and quotations

Isobel Carlson

A modest garden contains, for those who know how to look and to wait, more instruction than a library.

Henri Frédéric Amiel

Let us, then, begin by defining what a garden is, and what it ought to be. It is a piece of ground fenced off from cattle, and appropriated to the use and pleasure of man: it is or ought to be, cultivated and enriched by art, with such products as are not natural to this country, and, consequently, it must be artificial in its treatment, and may, without impropriety, be so in its appearance; yet, there is so much of littleness in art, when compared with nature, that they cannot well be blended; it were, therefore, to be wished, that the exterior of a garden should be made to assimilate with park scenery, or the landscape of nature; the interior may then be laid out with all the variety, contrast, and even whim, that can produce pleasing objects to the eye.

Humphry Repton,
Observations on the Theory and Practice of
Landscape Gardening

Garden Thoughts

The kiss of the sun for pardon,
The song of the birds for mirth,
One is nearer God's heart in a garden
Than anywhere else on earth.

Dorothy Frances Gurney

from The Feat of Gardening

How so well a gardener be,
Here he may both hear and see
Every time of the year and of the moon
And how the crafte shall be done,
In what manner he shall delve and set
Both in drought and in wet,
How he shall his seeds sow;
Of every month he must know
Both of wortes and of leek,
Onions and of garlic,
Parsley, clary and eke sage
And all other herbage.

John Gardner

You have heard it said that flowers only flourish rightly in the garden of someone who loves them. I know you would like that to be true; and would think it a pleasant magic if you could flush your flowers into brighter bloom by a kind look upon them.

John Ruskin, *Sesame and Lilies*

from Magdalen Walks

The little white clouds are racing over the sky,
    And the fields are strewn with the gold of the flower
       of March,
    The daffodil breaks under foot, and the tasselled larch
Sways and swings as the thrush goes hurrying by.

A delicate odour is borne on the wings
       of the morning breeze,
    The odour of deep wet grass, and of brown
       new-furrowed earth,
    The birds are singing for joy of the Spring's glad birth,
Hopping from branch to branch on the rocking trees.

And all the woods are alive with the murmur
     and sound of spring,
   And the rose bud breaks into pink on the climbing briar,
   And the crocus-bed is quivering moon of fire
Girdled round with the belt of an amethyst ring.

And the plane to the pine-tree is whispering some tale
     of love
   Till it rustles with laughter and tosses its mantle of green,
   And the gloom of the wych-elm's hollow is lit
     with the iris sheen
Of the burnished rainbow throat and the silver breast
     of a dove.

Oscar Wilde

It was the sweetest, most mysterious-looking place any one could imagine. The high walls which shut it in were covered with the leafless stems of climbing roses, which were so thick that they were matted together. Mary Lennox knew they were roses because she had seen a great many roses in India. All the ground was covered with grass of a wintry brown and out of it grew clumps of bushes which were surely rosebushes if they were alive. There were numbers of standard roses which had so spread their branches that they were like little trees. There were other trees in the garden, and one of the things which made the place look strangest and loveliest was that climbing roses had run all over them and swung down long tendrils which made light swaying curtains, and here and there they had caught at each other or at a far-reaching branch and had crept from one tree to another and made lovely bridges of themselves. There were neither leaves nor roses on them now and Mary did not know whether they were dead or alive, but their thin grey or brown branches and sprays looked like a sort of hazy mantle spreading over everything, walls, and trees, and even brown grass, where they had fallen from their fastenings and run along the ground. It was this hazy tangle from tree to tree which made it all look so mysterious. Mary had thought it must be different from other gardens which had not been left all by themselves so long; and indeed it was different from any other place she had ever seen in her life.

'How still it is!' she whispered. 'How still!'

Frances Hodgson Burnett,
The Secret Garden

How fair is a garden amid the toils
and passions of existence.

Benjamin Disraeli

They reached the flower-garden, and turned mechanically in at the gate that opened, through a high thick hedge, on an expanse of brilliant colour, which, after the green shades they had passed through, startled the eye like flames… the flowers were glowing wit their evening splendours; verbenas and heliotropes were sending up their finest incense. It seemed a gala where all was happiness and brilliancy, and misery could find no sympathy.

George Eliot, Scenes of Clerical Life

The Gardener wi' his Paidle

When rosy May comes in wi' flowers
To deck her gay, green, spreading bowers;
Then busy, busy are his hours,
    The gardener wi' his paidle.–

The crystal waters gently fa';
The merry birds are lovers a';
The scented breezes round him blaw,
    The gardener wi' his paidle.–

When purple morning starts the hare
To steal upon her early fare;
Then thro' the dews he maun repair,
    The gardener wi' his paidle.–

When Day, expiring in the west,
The curtain draws of Nature's rest;
He flies to her arms he lo'es the best,
    The gardener wi' his paidle.–

Robert Burns

He rambled an hour in breathless ecstasy, brushing the dew from the deep fern and bracken and the rich borders of the garden, tasting the fragrant air and stopping everywhere in murmuring rapture, at the touch of some exquisite impression. His whole walk was peopled with recognitions; he had been dreaming all his life of just such a place and such objects, such a morning and such a chance. It was the last of April and everything was fresh and vivid; the great trees in the early air, were a blur of tender shoots. Round the admirable house he revolved repeatedly, catching every aspect and feeling every value, feasting on the whole expression… There was something in the way the grey walls rose from the green lawn that brought tears to his eyes…

Henry James, The Princess Casamassima

'O Tiger-lily,' said Alice, addressing herself to one that was waving gracefully about in the wind, 'I *wish* you could talk!'

'We *can* talk,' said the Tiger-lily, 'when there's anybody worth talking to.'

Alice was so astonished that she couldn't speak for a minute: it quite seemed to take her breath away. At length, as the Tiger-lily only went on waving about, she spoke again, in a timid voice – almost in a whisper. 'And can *all* the flowers talk?'

'As well as *you* can,' said the Tiger-lily. 'And a great deal louder.'

'It isn't manners for us to begin, you know,' said the Rose, 'and I really was wondering when you'd speak! Said I to myself, "Her face has got *some* sense in it, though it's not a clever one!" Still, you're the right colour, and that goes a long way.'

'I don't care about the colour,' the Tiger-lily remarked. 'If only her petals curled up a little more, she'd be all right.'

Alice didn't like being criticised, so she began asking questions. 'Aren't you sometimes frightened at being planted out here, with nobody to take care of you?'

'There's the tree in the middle,' said the Rose. 'What else is it good for?'

Lewis Carroll, Through the Looking-glass

The Caterpillar

Brown and furry
Caterpillar in a hurry,
Take your walk
To the shady leaf, or stalk,
Or what not,
Which may be the chosen spot.
No toad spy you,
Hovering bird of prey pass by you:
Spin and die,
To live again a butterfly.

Christina Rossetti

A gap in the hedge gave a view into the gardens; a border of jasmine, pansies and verbena which ran along the wide path, was interplanted with fragrant wallflowers the faded rose of old Cordoba leather. A long green hose snaking across the gravel sent up every few yards a vertical, prismatic fan, and the multicoloured drops showered over the flowers in a perfumed cloud.

Marcel Proust, *Du Côté de chez Swann*

Robin

The sparrow seeks his feathers for a nest
And the fond robin with his ruddy breast
Hops round the garden wall were thickly twine
The leafing sweet briar and the propt woodbine
And in a hole behind the thickening boughs
He builds with hopeful joy his little house
Stealing with jealous speed the wool and hair
Were cows and sheep have lain them down to lair
And pecks the green moss in his murmuring glee
From cottage thatch and squatting apple tree
Tutling his song –

John Clare

What a desolate place would be a world without a flower! It would be a face without a smile, a feast without a welcome.

A. J. Balfour

In fine weather the old gentleman is almost constantly in the garden, and when it is too wet to go into it, he will look out of the window at it, by the hour together. He has always something to do there, and you will see him digging, and sweeping, and cutting, and planting, with manifest delight. In spring-time there is no end to the sowing of seeds, and sticking little bits of wood over them, with labels, which look like epitaphs to their memory; and in the evening, when the sun has gone down, the perseverance with which he lugs a great watering-pot about is perfectly astonishing…

Charles Dickens, Sketches by Boz

The Lily

The modest Rose puts forth a thorn,
The humble Sheep a threat'ning horn;
While the Lily white shall in love delight,
Nor a thorn, nor a threat, stain her beauty bright.

William Blake

from The Deserted Garden

I mind me in the days departed,
How often underneath the sun
With childish bounds I used to run
    To a garden long deserted.

The beds and walks were vanished quite;
And wheresoe'er had struck the spade,
The greenest grasses Nature laid
    To sanctify her right.

I called the place my wilderness,
For no one entered there but I;
The sheep looked in, the grass to espy,
    And passed it ne'ertheless.

The trees were interwoven wild,
And spread their boughs enough about
To keep both sheep and shepherd out,
But not a happy child.

Adventurous joy it was for me!
I crept beneath the boughs, and found
A circle smooth of mossy ground
Beneath a poplar tree.

Old garden rose-trees hedged it in,
Bedropt with roses waxen-white
Well satisfied with dew and light
And careless to be seen.

Elizabeth Barrett Browning

The moonbeams fell upon the roof and garden of Gerrard. It suffused the cottage with its brilliant light, except where the dark depth of the embowered porch defied its entry. All round the beds of flowers and herbs spread sparkling and defined. You could trace the minutest walk; almost distinguish every leaf. Now and then there came a breath, and the sweet-peas murmured in their sleep or the roses rustled, as if they were afraid they were about to be roused from their lightsome dreams. Further on the fruit trees caught the splendour of the night; and looked like a troop of sultanas taking their garden air, when the eye of man could not prophane them, and laden with jewels. There were apples that rivalled rubies; pears of topaz tint; a whole paraphernalia of plums, some purple as the amethyst, others blue and brilliant as the sapphire; an emerald here, and now a golden drop that gleamed like the yellow diamond of Genghis Khan.

Benjamin Disraeli, Sybil

from Upon Appleton House

See how the flowers, as at parade,
Under their colours stand displayed;
Each regiment in order grows,
That of the tulip, pink, and rose.
But when the vigilant patrol
Of stars walks round about the pole,
Their leaves that to the stalks are curled
Seem to their staves the ensigns furled.
Then in some flower's belovèd hut,
Each bee, as sentinel, is shut,
And sleeps so too, but, if once stirred,
She runs you through, nor asks the word.

Andrew Marvell

The Months

January brings the snow,
Makes our feet and fingers glow.

February brings the rain,
Thaws the frozen lake again.

March brings breezes loud and shrill,
Stirs the dancing daffodil.

April brings the primrose sweet,
Scatters daisies at our feet.

May brings flocks of pretty lambs,
Skipping by their fleecy dams.

June brings tulips, lilies, roses,
Fills the children's hands with posies.

Hot July brings cooling showers,
Apricots and gillyflowers.

August brings the sheaves of corn,
Then the harvest home is borne.

Warm September brings the fruit,
Sportsmen then begin to shoot.

Fresh October brings the pheasant,
Then to gather nuts is pleasant.

Dull November brings the blast,
Then the leaves are whirling fast.

Chill December brings the sleet,
Blazing fire, and Christmas treat.

Sara Coleridge

I value my garden more for being full of blackbirds than of cherries, and very frankly give them fruit for their songs.

Joseph Addison

A lovely warm sunny morning, the purple plumes of the silver birch fast thickening with buds waved and swayed gently in the soft spring air against the deep cloudless blue sky. The apricot blossoms were blowing and under the silver weeping birch the daffodils were dancing and nodding their golden heads in the morning wind and sunshine.

Rev Francis Kilvert

To Blossoms

Why do you fall so fast?
Your date is not so past,
But you may stay yet here awhile,
To blush and gently smile,
And go at last.

What! were ye born to be
An hour or half's delight,
And so to bid good night?
'Tis pity nature brought ye forth
Merely to show your worth,
And lose you quite.

But you are lovely leaves, where we
May read how soon things have
Their end, though ne'er so brave:
And after they have shown their pride,
Like you awhile, they glide
Into the grave.

Robert Herrick

The pride of my heart and the delight of my eyes is my garden… I know nothing so pleasant as to sit there on a summer afternoon, with the western sun flickering through the great elder-tree, and lighting up our gay parterres, where flowers and flowering shrubs are set as thick as grass in a field, a wilderness of blossom, interwoven, intertwined, wreathy, garlandy, profuse beyond all profusion, where we may guess that there is such a thing as mould, but never see it. I know nothing so pleasant as to sit in the shade of that dark bower, with the eye resting on that bright piece of colour, lighted so gloriously by the evening sun…

Mary Mitford, Our Village

Digging

Today I think
Only with scents, — scents dead leaves yield,
And bracken, and wild carrot's seed,
And the square mustard field;

Odours that rise
When the spade wounds the root of tree,
Rose, currant, raspberry, or goutweed,
Rhubarb or celery;

The smoke's smell, too,
Flowing from where a bonfire burns
The dead, the waste, the dangerous,
And all to sweetness turns.

It is enough
To smell, to crumble the dark earth,
While the robin sings over again
Sad songs of Autumn mirth.

Edward Thomas

from Ah! Sun-flower!

Ah, Sun-flower! weary of time,
Who countest the steps of the Sun:
Seeking after that sweet golden clime,
Where the traveller's journey is done.

William Blake

If well managed, nothing is more beautiful than the kitchen garden: the earliest blossoms come there: we shall in vain seek for flowering shrubs in March, and early in April, to equal the peaches, nectarines, apricots and plums; late in April, we shall find nothing to equal the pear and the cherry; and, in May, the dwarf, or espalier, apple-trees, are just so many immense garlands of carnations.

William Cobbett, *The English Gardener*

Now I am in the garden at the back… – a very preserve of butterflies, as I remember it, with a high fence, and a gate and padlock; where the fruit clusters on the trees, riper and richer than fruit has ever been since, in any other garden, and where my mother gathers some in a basket, while I stand by, bolting furtive gooseberries, and trying to look unmoved.

Charles Dickens, David Copperfield

I know that if odour were visible, as colour is, I'd see the summer garden in rainbow clouds.

Robert Bridges, 'The Testament of Beauty'

The Gardener

The gardener does not love to talk,
He makes me keep the gravel walk;
And when he puts his tools away,
He locks the door and takes the key.

Away behind the currant row
Where no one else but cook may go,
Far in the plots, I see him dig,
Old and serious, brown and big.

He digs the flowers, green, red, and blue,
Nor wishes to be spoken to.
He digs the flowers and cuts the hay,
And never seems to want to play.

Silly gardener! summer goes,
And winter comes with pinching toes,
When in the garden bare and brown
You must lay your barrow down.

Well now, and while the summer stays,
To profit by these garden days,
O how much wiser you would be
To play at Indian wars with me!

Robert Louis Stevenson

The garden is best to be square; encompassed, on all the four sides, with a stately arched hedge. The arches to be upon pillars of carpenter's work, of some ten foot high and six foot broad; and the spaces between of the same dimension with the breadth of the arch. Over the arches let there be an entire hedge, of some four foot high, framed also upon carpenter's work; and upon the upper hedge, over every arch, a little turret, with a belly, enough to receive a cage of birds; and over every space between the arches some other little figure, with broad plates of round coloured glass, gilt, for the sun to play upon. But this hedge I intend to be raised upon a bank, not steep, but gently slope, of some six foot, set all with flowers. Also I understand that this square of the garden should not be the whole breadth of the ground, but to leave, on either side, ground enough for diversity of side alleys; unto which the two covert alleys

of the green may deliver you. But there must be no alleys with hedges at either end of this great enclosure: not at the hither end, for letting your prospect upon this fair hedge from the green; nor at the further end, for letting your prospect from the hedge, through the arches, upon the heath.

Sir Francis Bacon, 'Of Gardens'

from The Garden in September

Now thin mists temper the slow-ripening beams
Of the September sun: his golden gleams
On gaudy flowers shine, that prank the rows
Of high-grown hollyhocks, and all tall shows
That Autumn flaunteth in his bushy bowers;
Where tomtits, hanging from the drooping heads
Of giant sunflowers, peck the nutty seeds;
And in the feathery aster bees on wing
Seize and set free the honied flowers,
Till thousand stars leap with their visiting:
While ever across the path mazily flit,
Unpiloted in the sun,
The dreamy butterflies
With dazzling colours powdered and soft glooms,
White, black and crimson stripes, and peacock eyes,
Or on chance flowers sit,
With idle effort plundering one by one
The nectaries of deepest-throated blooms.

With gentle flaws the western breeze
Into the garden saileth,
Scarce here and there stirring the single trees,
For his sharpness he vaileth:
So long a comrade of the bearded corn,
Now from the stubbles whence the shocks are borne,
O'er dewy lawns he turns to stray,
As mindful of the kisses and soft play
Wherewith he enamoured the light-hearted May,
Ere he deserted her;
Lover of fragrance, and too late repents;
Nor more of heavy hyacinth now may drink,
Nor spicy pink,
Nor summer's rose, nor garnered lavender,
But the few lingering scents
Of streaked pea, and gillyflower, and stocks
Of courtly purple, and aromatic phlox.

Robert Bridges

The patch of land he had made into a garden was famous in the town for the beauty of the flowers which he grew there… By dint of hard work, constant care, and endless buckets of water, he had even become a creator, inventing certain tulips and dahlias which seemed to have been forgotten by nature.

Victor Hugo, *Les Misérables*

What is Pink?

What is pink? A rose is pink
By the fountain's brink.
What is red? A poppy's red
In its barley bed.
What is blue? The sky is blue
Where the clouds float through.
What is white? A swan is white
Sailing in the light.
What is yellow? Pears are yellow,
Rich and ripe and mellow.
What is green? The grass is green
With small flowers between.
What is violet? Clouds are violet
In the summer twilight.
What is orange? Why, an orange,
Just an orange!

Christina Rossetti

It is a greater act of faith to plant a bulb than to plant a tree… to see in these wizened, colourless shapes the subtle curves of the iris reticulata or the tight locks of the hyacinth.

Claire Leighton, *Four Hedges*

How beautiful a garden is when all the fruit-trees are in bloom, and how various that bloom is! Each Pear-tree bears a different blossom from its neighbour, and the handsomest of all, in size and shape of flower and form of cluster, is the Jargonelle. But no Pear-blossom can compare with the beauty of blossom on the Apple-trees; and of all Apple-trees the Pomeroy is most beautiful, when every bough is laden with clusters of deep-red buds, which shade off into the softest rosy white as, one by one, the blossoms open out.

Henry Bright,
A Year in a Lancashire Garden

The Kitten at Play

See the kitten on the wall,
Sporting with the leaves that fall,
Withered leaves – one, two, and three –
From the lofty elder tree!
Through the calm and frosty air
Of this morning bright and fair,
Eddying round and round they sink
Softly, slowly: one might think
From the motions that are made,
Every little leaf conveyed

Sylph or faery hither tending,
To this lower world descending,
Each invisible and mute,
In his wavering parachute.
– But the kitten, how she starts,
Crouches, stretches, paws, and darts!
First at one, and then its fellow,
Just as light and just as yellow;
There are many now – now one –
Now they stop; and there are none.

William Wordsworth

My Neighbor's Roses

The roses red upon my neighbor's vine
Are owned by him, but they are also mine.
His was the cost, and his the labor, too,
But mine as well as his the joy, their loveliness to view.

They bloom for me and are for me as fair
As for the man who gives them all his care.
Thus I am rich, because a good man grew
A rose-clad vine for all his neighbors' view.

I know from this that others plant for me,
And what they own, my joy may also be.
So why be selfish, when so much that's fine
Is grown for you, upon your neighbor's vine.

Abraham L. Gruber

There are, besides the temper of our climate, two things particular to us, that contribute much to the beauty and elegance of our gardens, which are the gravel of our walks, and the fineness and almost perpetual greenness of our turf. The first is not known anywhere else, which leaves all their dry walks in other countries, very unpleasant and uneasy. The other cannot be found in France or in Holland as we have it, the soil not admitting that fineness of blade in Holland, nor the sun that greenness in France, during most of the summer; nor indeed is it to be found but in the finest of our soils.

Sir William Temple

The Daisy

The daisy is a happy flower,
    And comes at early spring,
And brings with it the sunny hour
    When bees are on the wing.

It brings with it the butterfly,
    And early humble-bee;
With the polyanthus' golden eye,
    And blooming apple-tree;

Hedge-sparrows from the mossy nest
    In the old garden hedge,
Where schoolboys, in their idle glee,
    Seek pooties as their pledge.

The cow stands browsing all the day
    Over the orchard gate,
And eats her bit of sweet old hay;
    And Goody stands to wait,

Lest what's not eaten the rude wind
    May rise and snatch away
Over the neighbour's hedge behind,
    Where hungry cattle lay.

John Clare

My flowers grow up in several parts of the garden in the greatest luxuriancy and profusion... if I meet with any one in a field which pleases me, I give it a place in my garden. By this means, when a stranger walks with me, he is surprised to see large spots of ground covered with ten thousand different colours, and has often singled out flowers he might have met with under a common hedge, in a field, or in a meadow, as some of the greatest beauties of the place... I take in none that do not naturally rejoice in the soil, and am pleased, when I am walking, in a labyrinth of my own raising, not to know whether the next tree I shall meet with is an apple or an oak; an elm or a pear tree.

Joseph Addison

There is no gardening without humility. Nature is constantly sending even its oldest scholars to the bottom of the class for some egregious blunder.

Alfred Austin

A Contemplation Upon Flowers

Brave flowers – that I could gallant it like you,
    And be as little vain!
You come abroad, and make a harmless show,
    And to your beds of earth again.
You are not proud: you know your birth:
For your embroider'd garments are from earth.

You do obey your months and times, but I
    Would have it ever Spring:
My fate would know no Winter, never die,
    Nor think of such a thing.
O that I could my bed of earth but view
And smile, and look as cheerfully as you!

O teach me to see Death and not to fear,
　　But rather to take truce!
How often have I seen you at bier,
　　And there look fresh and spruce!
You fragrant flowers! then teach me, that my breath
Like yours may sweeten and perfume my death.

Henry King

from Hortulus

Though a life of retreat offers various joys,
None, I think, will compare with the time one employs
In the study of herbs, or in striving to gain
Some practical knowledge of nature's domain.
Get a garden! What kind you may get matters not.

Abbot Walafrid Strabo

While such honey-dew fell, such silence reigned, such gloaming gathered, I felt as if I could haunt such shade for ever: but in threading the flower and fruit-parterres at the upper part of the inclosure, enticed there by the light the now-risen moon casts on this more open quarter, my step is stayed – not by sound, not by sight, but once more by a warning fragrance.

Sweet briar and southernwood, jasmine, pink, and rose, have long been yielding their evening sacrifice of incense: this new scent is neither of shrub nor flower; it is – I know it well – it is Mr Rochester's cigar.

Charlotte Brontë, Jane Eyre

On Pruning

Proud of his well-spread walls, he views his trees
That meet (no barren interval between)
With pleasure more than ev'n their fruits afford,
Which, save himself who trains them, none can feel:
These, therefore, are his own peculiar charge;
No meaner hand may disciple the shoots,
None but his steel approach them. What is weak,
Distemper'd, or has lost prolific pow'rs,
Impair'd by age, his unrelenting hand
Dooms to the knife: nor does he spare the soft
And succulent, that feeds its giant growth,

But barren, at th' expence of neighb'ring twigs
Less ostentatious, and yet studded thick
With hopeful gems. The rest, no portion left
That may disgrace his art, or disappoint
Large expectation, he disposes neat
At measur'd distances, that air and sun,
Admitted freely, may afford their aid,
And ventilate and warm the swelling buds.
Hence summer has her riches, autumn hence,
And hence ev'n winter fills his wither'd hand
With blushing fruits, and plenty, not his own.

William Cowper

A half-moon, dusky gold, was sinking behind the black sycamore at the end of the garden, making the sky dull purple with its glow. Nearer, a dim white fence of lilies went across the garden, and the air all round seemed to stir with scent… He went across the beds of pinks, whose keen perfume came sharply across the rocking, heavy scent of the lilies, and stood alongside the white barrier of flowers. They flagged all loose, as if they were panting. The scent made him drunk.

D. H. Lawrence, *Sons and Lovers*

Trees

I think that I shall never see
A poem as lovely as a tree.

A tree whose hungry mouth is pressed
Against the earth's sweet flowing breast;

A tree that looks at God all day,
And lifts her leafy arms to pray;

A tree that may in summer wear
A nest of robins in her hair;

Upon whose bosom snow has lain;
Who intimately lives with rain.

Poems are made by fools like me,
But only God can make a tree.

Joyce Kilmer

The garden is never dead; growth is always going on, and growth that can be seen, and seen with delight.

Henry Ellacombe,
In My Vicarage Garden

Mr Collins invited them to take a stroll in the garden, which was large and well laid out, and to the cultivation of which he attended himself. To work in his garden was one of his most respectable pleasures... Here, leading the way through every walk and cross walk, and scarcely allowing them an interval to utter the praises he asked for, every view was pointed out with a minuteness which left beauty entirely behind.

Jane Austen, *Pride and Prejudice*

The Garden Seat

Its former green is blue and thin,
And its once firm legs sink in and in,
Soon it will break down unaware,
Soon it will break down unaware.

At night when reddest flowers are black,
Those who once sat thereon come back;
Quite a row of them sitting there,
Quite a row of them sitting there.

With them the seat does not break down,
Nor winter freeze them, nor floods drown.
For they are as light as upper air,
For they are as light as upper air!

Thomas Hardy

There were the smoothest lawns in the world stretching down to the edge of the liquid slowness and making, where the water touched them, a line as even as the rim of a champagne glass… The place was a garden of delight.

Henry James, *English Hours*

from On a Fine Crop of Peas being Spoiled by a Storm

When Morrice views his prostrate peas,
    By raging whirlwhinds spread,
He wrings his hands, and in amaze
    He sadly shakes his head.

'Is this the fruit of my fond toil,
    My joy, my pride, my cheer!
Shall one tempestuous hour thus spoil
    The labours of a year!

Oh! what avails, that day to day
    I nursed the thriving crop,
And settled with my foot the clay,
    And reared the social prop!

Ambition's pride had spurred me on
    All gard'ners to excell.
I often called them one by one,
    And boastingly would tell,

How I prepared the furrowed ground
    And how the grain did sow,
Then challenged all the country round
    For such an early blow.

How did their bloom my wishes raise!
    What hopes did they afford,
To earn my honoured master's praise,
    And crown his cheerful board!'

Poor Morrice, wrapt in sad surprise,
    Demands in sober mood,
'Should storms molest a man so wise,
    A man so just and good?'

Ah! Morrice, cease thy fruitless moan,
    Nor at misfortunes spurn,
Misfortune's not thy lot alone;
    Each neighbour hath his turn.

Henry Jones

Upon a Snail

She goes but softly, but she goeth sure;
She stumbles not, as stronger creatures do;
Her journey's shorter, so she may endure
Better than they which do much farther go.
She makes no noise, but stilly seizeth on
The flower or herb appointed for her food,
The which she quietly doth feed upon,
While others range and glare, but find no good.
And though she doth but very softly go,
However 'tis not fast, nor slow, but sure;
And certainly they that do travel so,
The prize they do aim at they do procure.

John Bunyan

When the world wearies, and society ceases to satisfy, there is always the garden.

Minnie Aumônier

Every afternoon, as they were coming from school, the children used to go and play in the Giant's garden.

It was a large lovely garden, with soft green grass. Here and there over the grass stood beautiful flowers like stars, and there were twelve peach-trees that in the spring-time broke out into delicate blossoms of pink and pearl, and in the autumn bore rich fruit. The birds sat on the trees and sang so sweetly that the children used to stop their games in order to listen to them. 'How happy we are here!' they cried to each other.

Oscar Wilde,
The Happy Prince and Other Tales

Flowers have an expression of countenance as much as men or animals. Some seem to smile; some have a sad expression; some are pensive and diffident; others again are plain, honest and upright, like the broad-faced sunflower and the hollyhock.

Henry Ward Beecher

from The Planting of the Apple-Tree

Come, let us plant the apple-tree.
Cleave the tough greensward with the spade
Wide let its hollow bed be made;
There gently lay the roots, and there
Sift the dark mould with kindly care,
And press it o'er them tenderly,
As, round the sleeping infant's feet,
We softly fold the cradle-sheet;
So plant we the apple-tree.

What plant we in this apple-tree?
Buds, which the breath of summer days
Shall lengthen into leafy sprays;
Boughs where the thrush, with crimson breast,
Shall haunt and sing and hide her nest;
We plant, upon the sunny lea,
A shadow for the noontide hour,
A shelter from the summer shower,
When we plant the apple-tree.

What plant we in this apple-tree?
Sweets for a hundred flowery springs
To load the May-wind's restless wings,
When, from the orchard row, he pours
Its fragrance through our open doors;
A world of blossoms for the bee,
Flowers for the sick girl's silent room,
For the glad infant sprigs of bloom,
We plant with the apple-tree.

What plant we in this apple-tree?
Fruits that shall swell in sunny June,
And redden in the August noon,
And drop, when gentle airs come by,
That fan the blue September sky,
While children come, with cries of glee,
And seek them where the fragrant grass
Betrays their bed to those who pass,
At the foot of the apple-tree.

William Cullen Bryant

Large or small, the garden should look both orderly and rich. It should be well fenced from the outer world. It should by no means imitate either the wilfulness or the wildness of Nature, but should look like a thing never seen except near a house.

William Morris,
Hopes and Fears for Art

from The Nymph Complaining for the Death of her Faun

I have a garden of my own,
But so with roses overgrown
And lilies, that you would it guess
To be a little wilderness.

Andrew Marvell

How beautiful the whole garden looked at the hour when it should have been night, about ten o'clock, in the strange, weirdly daylight! Beyond the high west line of wall and the trees at the upper end, in the cold clear sky lay level flakes of cloud, fired by a sunset glow.

E. V. Boyle,
Sylvana's Letters to an Unknown Friend

To a Bed of Tulips

Bright Tulips, we do know,
You had your comming hither;
And Fading-time do's show,
That Ye must quickly wither.

Your *Sister-hoods* may stay,
And smile here for your houre;
But dye ye must away:
Even as the meanest Flower.

Come Virgins then, and see
Your frailties; and bemone ye;
For lost like these, 'twill be,
As Time had never known ye.

Robert Herrick

The many great gardens of the world, of literature and poetry, of painting and music, of religion and architecture, all make the point as clear as possible: the soul cannot thrive in the absence of a garden.

Thomas Moore

I used to visit and revisit it a dozen times a day, and stand in deep contemplation over my vegetable progeny with a love that nobody could share or conceive of who had never taken part in the process of creation. It was one of the most bewitching sights in the world to observe a hill of beans thrusting aside the soil, or a rose of early peas just peeping forth sufficiently to trace a line of delicate green.

Nathaniel Hawthorne,
Mosses from an Old Manse

The Blackbird

O blackbird! Sing me something well:
    While all the neighbours shoot thee round,
    I keep smooth plats of fruitful ground,
Where thou may'st warble, eat and dwell.

The espaliers and the standards all
    Are thine; the range of lawn and park:
    The unnetted black-hearts ripen dark,
All thine, against the garden wall.

Yet, tho' I spared thee all the spring,
    Thy sole delight is, sitting still,
    With that gold dagger of thy bill
To fret the summer jenneting.

A golden bill! the silver tongue,
   Cold February loved, is dry:
   Plenty corrupts the melody
That made thee famous once, when young:

And in the sultry garden-squares,
   Now thy flute-notes are changed to coarse,
   I hear thee not at all, or hoarse
As when a hawker hawks his wares.

Take warning! he that will not sing
   While yon sun prospers in the blue,
   Shall sing for want, ere leaves are new,
Caught in the frozen palms of Spring.

Alfred Tennyson

Being thus prepared for us in all ways, and made beautiful, and good for food, and for building, and for instruments of our hands, this race of plants, deserving boundless affection and admiration from us, becomes, in proportion to their obtaining it, a nearly perfect test of our being in right temper of mind and way of life; so that no one can be far wrong in either who loves trees enough, and everyone is assuredly wrong in both who does not love them, if his life has brought them in his way.

John Ruskin, Modern Painters

I think the true gardener is a lover of his flowers, not a critic of them. I think the true gardener is the reverent servant of Nature, not her truculent, wife-beating master. I think the true gardener, the older he grows, should more and more develop a humble, grateful and uncertain spirit.

Reginald Farrer, *In a Yorkshire Garden*

Hence we went to Swallowfield; this house is after the ancient building of honourable gentlemen's houses, when they kept up ancient hospitality, but the gardens and waters as elegant as 'tis possible to make a flat, by art and industry, and no mean expense, my lady being so extraordinarily skilled in the flowery part, and my lord in diligence of planting; so that I have hardly seen a seat which shows more tokens of it than what is to be found here, not only in the delicious and rarest fruits of a garden, but in those innumerable timber trees in the ground about the seat, to the greatest ornament and benefit of the place. There is one orchard of 1000 golden, and other cider pippins; walks and groves of elms, limes, oaks, and other trees. The garden is so beset with all manners of sweet shrubs, that it perfumes the air. The distribution also of the quarters, walks, and parterres, is excellent. The nurseries, kitchen garden full of the most desirable plants; two very noble Orangeries well furnished; but above all, the canal and fishponds, the one fed with a white, the other with a black running water, fed by a quick and swift river, so well and plentifully stored with fish, that for pike, carp, bream and tench, I never saw anything approaching it.

John Evelyn

from The Glory of the Garden

Our England is a garden that is full of stately views,
Of borders, beds and shrubberies and lawns and avenues,
With statues on the terraces and peacocks strutting by;
But the Glory of the Garden lies in more than meets the eye.

For where the old thick laurels grow along the thin red wall,
You will find the tool- and potting-sheds which are the heart of all;
The cold-frames and the hot-houses, the dungpits and the tanks,
The rollers, carts and drain-pipes, with the barrows and the planks.

And there you'll see the gardeners, the men and prentice boys
Told off to do as they are bid and do it without noise:
For, except when seeds are planted and we shout to scare the birds,
The Glory of the Garden it abideth not in words.

And some can pot begonias and some can bud a rose,
And some are hardly fit to trust with anything that grows:
But they can roll and trim the lawns and sift the sand and loam,
For the Glory of the Garden occupieth all who come.

Our England is a garden, and such gardens are not made
By singing: – 'Oh, how beautiful!' and sitting in the shade,
While better men than we go out and start their working lives
At grubbing weeds from gravel-paths with broken dinner-knives.

There's not a pair of legs so thin, there's not a head so thick,
There's not a hand so weak and white, nor yet a heart so sick,
But it can find some needful job that's crying to be done,
For the Glory of the Garden glorifieth everyone.

Rudyard Kipling

An October Garden

In my Autumn garden I was fain
    To mourn among my scattered roses;
    Alas for that last rosebud that uncloses
To Autumn's languid sun and rain
When all the world is on the wane!
    Which has not felt the sweet constraint of June,
    Nor heard the nightingale in tune.

Broad-faced asters by my garden walk,
    You are but coarse compared with roses:
    More choice, more dear that rosebud which
        uncloses,
Faint-scented, pinched, upon its stalk,
That least and last which cold winds balk;
    A rose it is though least and last of all,
    A rose to me though at the fall.

Christina Rossetti

My greenhouse is never so pleasant as when we are just on the point of being turned out of it. The gentleness of the autumnal suns, and the calmness of this latter season, make it a much more agreeable retreat than we ever find it in summer… I sit with all the windows and door wide open, and am regaled with the scent of every flower in a garden as full of flowers as I have known how to make it.

William Cowper to Rev John Newton, 18 September 1784

www.summersdale.com